SCIENTIFIC AMERICAN | EDUCATIONAL PUBLISHING

SCIENTIFIC AMERICAN INVESTIGATES CAREERS IN SCIENCE
MICROBIOLOGIST

BY MEGAN QUICK

Published in 2026 by The Rosen Publishing Group
in association with Scientific American Educational Publishing
2544 Clinton Street, Buffalo NY 14224

Copyright © 2026 Rosen Publishing Group

Library of Congress Cataloging-in-Publication Data
Names: Quick, Megan author
Title: Microbiologist / Megan Quick.
Description: Buffalo, New York : Scientific American Educational
   Publishing, an imprint of Rosen Publishing, [2026] | Series: Scientific
   American investigates careers in science | Includes index. | Audience
   term: juvenile | Audience: Grades 4-6 Scientific American Educational
   Publishing, an imprint of Rosen Publishing
Identifiers: LCCN 2025002182 (print) | LCCN 2025002183 (ebook) | ISBN
   9781725352629 (library binding) | ISBN 9781725352612 (paperback) | ISBN
   9781725352636 (ebook)
Subjects: LCSH: Microbiologists–Juvenile literature |
   Microbiology–Vocational guidance–Juvenile literature
Classification: LCC QR57 .Q53 2026 (print) | LCC QR57 (ebook) | DDC
   579.023–dc23/eng/20250211
LC record available at https://lccn.loc.gov/2025002182
LC ebook record available at https://lccn.loc.gov/2025002183

Designer: Leslie Taylor
Editor: Megan Quick

Portions of this work were originally authored by Zelda Salt and published as *Be a Microbiologist*. All new material in this edition is authored by Megan Quick.

Photo credits: Cover (main) DC Studio/Shutterstock.com; series art (background) jijomathaidesigners/Shutterstock.com; p. 5 Gorodenkoff/Shutterstock.com; p. 7 BigBearCamera/Shutterstock.com; p. 8 Farknot Architect/Shutterstock.com; p. 9 I-ing/Shutterstock.com; p. 11 Kateryna Kon/Shutterstock.com; p. 13 angellodeco/Shutterstock.com; p. 15 PeopleImages.com - Yuri A/Shutterstock.com; p. 17 SANDIP NEOGI/Shutterstock.com; p. 18 AnaLysiSStudiO/Shutterstock.com; p. 19 Microgen/Shutterstock.com; p. 21 Stenoell/ File:Microbiological sampling on Mt. Erebus.jpg _commons.wikimedia.org; p. 23 Victor Ivin/Shutterstock.com; p. 25 NASA Johnson Space Center/File:Iss071e580478 (Aug. 29, 2024) — NASA astronauts Tracy C. Dyson (foreground) and Butch Wilmore wear personal protective equipment.jpg_commons.wikimedia.org; p. 27 Max Acronym/Shutterstock.com; p. 29 aslysun/Shutterstock.com.

Some of the images in this book illustrate individuals who are models. The depictions do not imply actual situations or events.

All rights reserved. No part of this book may be reproduced in any form without permission in writing from the publisher, except by a reviewer.

Printed in the United States of America

CPSIA compliance information: Batch #CSSA26. For Further Information contact Rosen Publishing at 1-800-237-9932.

CONTENTS

TINY BUT MIGHTY 4
MEET THE MICROBES 6
MICROBIOLOGISTS AT WORK 10
DISEASE FIGHTERS 12
ANIMAL MEDICINE 14
SAVING THE EARTH 16
MICROBES ON THE MENU 18
EXTREME MICROBIOLOGISTS 20
MARINE MICROBIOLOGISTS 22
SPACE MICROBES 24
SCHOOL DAYS 26
A BIG JOB 28
GLOSSARY 30
FOR MORE INFORMATION 31
INDEX 32

Words in the glossary appear in **bold** type the first time they are used in the text.

TINY BUT MIGHTY

Did you know that you have trillions of tiny **organisms** living on and in your body? They're called microorganisms, and they're so small that they can only be seen with a **microscope**. But don't worry! While some microorganisms can make you sick, most aren't harmful. In fact, many of them help you stay healthy.

Microbiologists study how microorganisms affect our bodies as well as the world around us. They look for ways to protect humans from diseases. Microbiologists also use what they know of these organisms to fight **climate change** and search for life on other planets. It's an exciting time to be a microbiologist!

Microbiologists use technology like computers and powerful microscopes to study tiny microorganisms.

MEET THE MICROBES

Microbes are microorganisms that cause disease or **fermentation**. A few of the most common ones are bacteria, fungi, and viruses.

Bacteria are organisms made of one cell that doesn't have many of the parts that cells normally have. Bacteria come in many shapes, such as rods, spheres, and spirals.

Bacteria are everywhere! They are in our bodies and in the ground, water, and air. Some bacteria help us digest, or break down, our food. They also break down matter in soil that can be used by plants. Other bacteria, known as pathogens, can make us sick by releasing harmful substances.

FUN FACT

THE HUMAN BODY CONTAINS MORE BACTERIA CELLS THAN HUMAN CELLS! SCIENTISTS ESTIMATE THAT THE AVERAGE HUMAN HAS 38 TRILLION BACTERIA CELLS AND 30 TRILLION HUMAN CELLS.

Bacteria Shapes

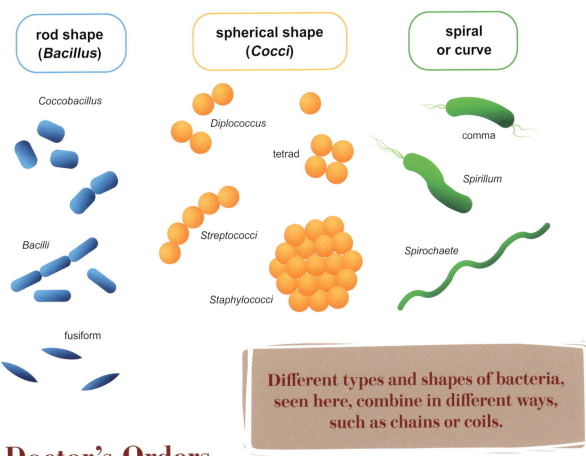

Different types and shapes of bacteria, seen here, combine in different ways, such as chains or coils.

Doctor's Orders

Chances are that you've been sick and taken antibiotics to get better. Antibiotics kill harmful bacteria or stop them from multiplying. Dr. Alexander Fleming discovered penicillin, the first antibiotic, in 1928. He found **mold** growing on a bacteria sample and realized a chemical in the mold was keeping the bacteria from growing. He named the chemical penicillin.

Fungi include molds, yeast, and mushrooms. Fungi feed on other organisms, such as dead plants and animals. Like bacteria, they can help plants by breaking down matter in the soil. Most fungi produce spores, which are tiny cells that become new fungi when they are released.

Viruses are **germs** that can make you sick. They are much smaller than both bacteria and fungi. A virus cannot survive on its own. Instead, it takes over a healthy cell and sends a message to the cell to make copies of the virus. These new viruses then leave that cell and spread to others.

FUN FACT

WE BITE INTO FUNGI EVERY TIME WE EAT BREAD. YEAST IS USED IN DOUGH TO MAKE IT RISE. THE YEAST EATS SUGAR AND RELEASES THE GAS CARBON DIOXIDE, MAKING THE DOUGH SOFT AND PUFFY.

8

Clumps of mold spores, like those on this bread, are known as colonies.

Mold Attack

Have you ever wondered why bread gets moldy? Bread contains starch, which mold feeds on. Mold is also attracted to moist bread that's stored in a cool, dark place. Tiny mold spores float all around the air. Once the spores land on the bread, they multiply quickly. Mold especially likes white bread!

MICROBIOLOGISTS AT WORK

A microbiologist may study any of the different types of microorganisms. They often work with bacteria, since they are so common and play so many roles, both good and bad.

Microbiologists study bacteria with the aid of lab tools such as microscopes and advanced computer systems that help **identify** bacteria. They often spend long hours in labs. Microbiologists might spend time testing different kinds of bacteria to see how they change in different temperatures. Or they might study bacteria samples to learn what conditions contribute to their growth. Microbiologists usually focus on one area, such as animals, the **environment**, or medicine.

FUN FACT

NOT ALL MICROORGANISMS REQUIRE A MICROSCOPE TO BE SEEN! THE LARGEST BACTERIUM IS CALLED *THIOMARGARITA MAGNIFICA* AND MEASURES ABOUT 0.4 INCH (1 CM) LONG.

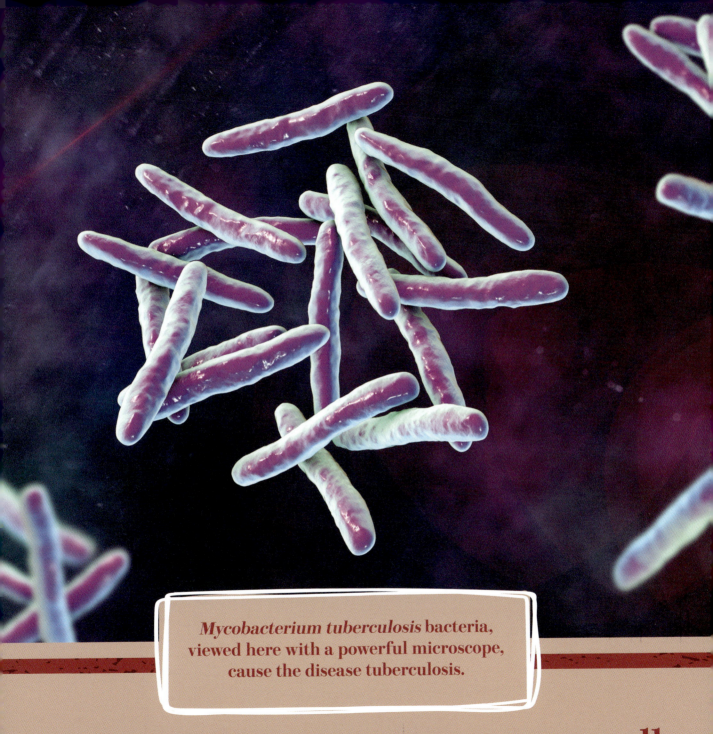

Mycobacterium tuberculosis bacteria, viewed here with a powerful microscope, cause the disease tuberculosis.

DISEASE FIGHTERS

Many diseases are caused by bacteria, viruses, or fungi. Medical microbiologists advise doctors who are **diagnosing** and treating infectious diseases. An infection is the spread of germs inside the body, causing illness. The medical microbiologist's role is to identify the bacteria causing the infection. Then, the microbiologist can advise the doctors of the best way to treat the infection and prevent further ones.

Medical microbiologists may work in hospitals or labs. They study and test microbes using powerful microscopes and other high-tech equipment. They look at samples from patients to learn which microbe is causing a disease and then find a way to treat it.

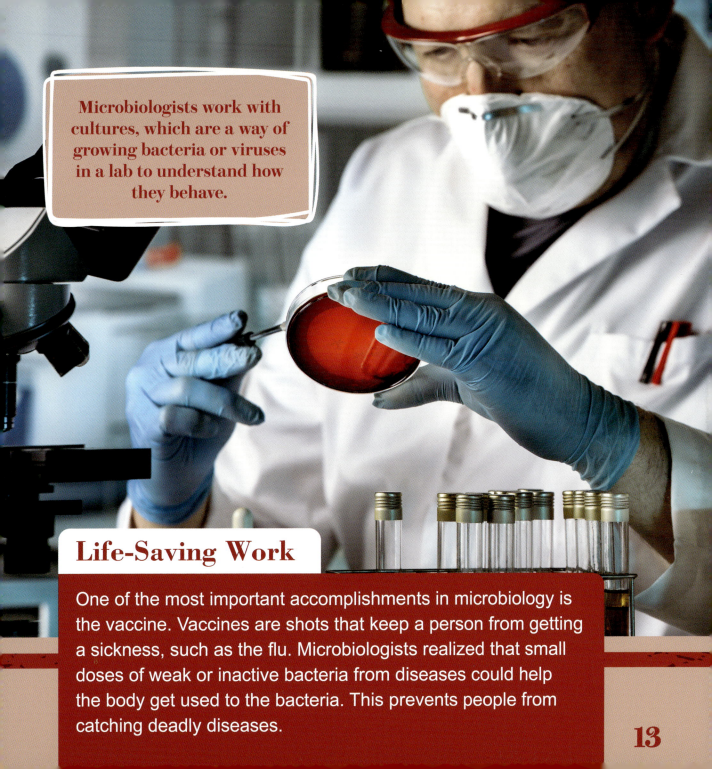

Microbiologists work with cultures, which are a way of growing bacteria or viruses in a lab to understand how they behave.

Life-Saving Work

One of the most important accomplishments in microbiology is the vaccine. Vaccines are shots that keep a person from getting a sickness, such as the flu. Microbiologists realized that small doses of weak or inactive bacteria from diseases could help the body get used to the bacteria. This prevents people from catching deadly diseases.

ANIMAL MEDICINE

A microbiologist's work is not limited to humans. Veterinary, or vet, microbiologists do much of the same work as medical microbiologists, but they focus on pets, farm animals, and other wildlife. They are often part of teams that develop medicines for animals.

Some diseases, such as rabies, can be passed from an infected animal to humans. These diseases can be very dangerous or even deadly. A vet microbiologist might work with vets and other doctors to diagnose and treat the disease.

Vet microbiologists don't usually work directly with animals. Instead, they spend time in labs, developing vaccines and medicines, and diagnosing diseases.

Vet microbiologists develop vaccines that keep pets and farm animals free from disease.

SAVING THE EARTH

A growing branch of microbiology focuses on protecting our planet. Rising temperatures, melting polar ice, and **extreme** weather are all part of climate change. A major cause of these changes is greenhouse gases, such as carbon dioxide, in the atmosphere. Many greenhouse gases come from human activity, but microbes in the soil and water also produce lots of carbon dioxide and other gases.

Environmental microbiologists study how microorganisms interact with the environment. In the case of global warming, they study how microbes in the soil, water, and animal waste produce gases. They can then figure out ways to reduce the amount of gases released into the atmosphere.

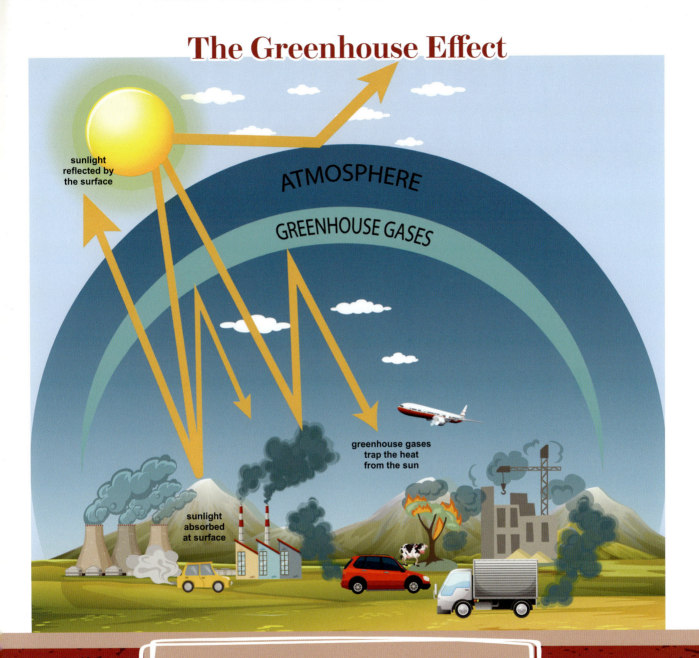

MICROBES ON THE MENU

Some bacteria and other microbes in food can make us sick. Food microbiologists study how these pathogens get into our food in order to prevent it from happening. They study food samples and test them to see if they contain harmful bacteria such as salmonella and listeria. Food microbiologists also make sure that food companies follow rules for food safety.

Food microbiologists can also use microbes to make sure your food tastes great! Microbes like bacteria and yeast play an important role in the flavor of our foods. Microbiologists pair microbes with different foods, testing combinations to get the best possible taste.

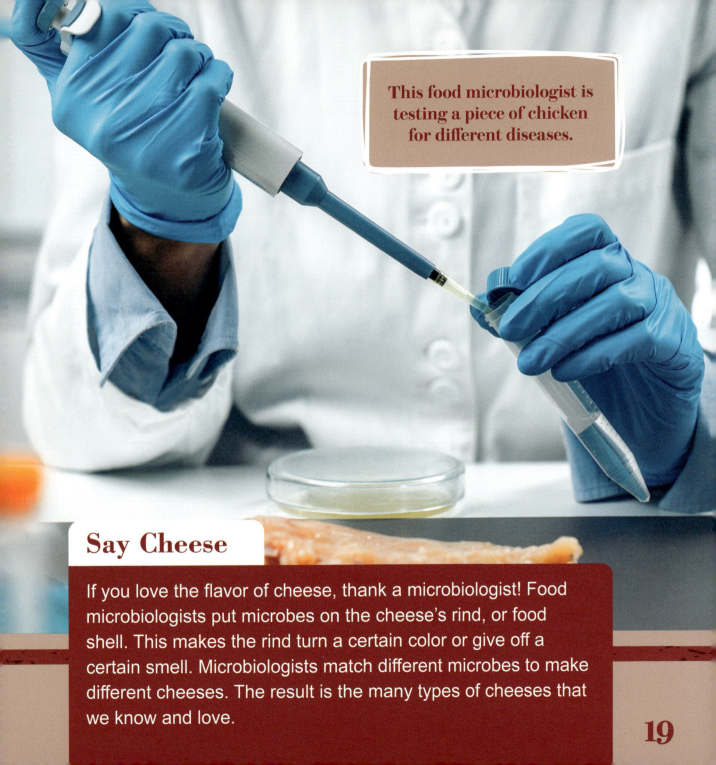

This food microbiologist is testing a piece of chicken for different diseases.

Say Cheese

If you love the flavor of cheese, thank a microbiologist! Food microbiologists put microbes on the cheese's rind, or food shell. This makes the rind turn a certain color or give off a certain smell. Microbiologists match different microbes to make different cheeses. The result is the many types of cheeses that we know and love.

EXTREME MICROBIOLOGISTS

Some microbiologists leave the lab behind and travel to faraway places. They often go to some of the highest, hottest, or coldest places on Earth.

The whole planet is covered in microbes, waiting to be discovered. A microbiologist can find microbes known as extremophiles in interesting places, like in oil wells and clouds! Microbes also live in extreme environments, such as ice fields and on the rims of **volcanoes**.

Microbiologists looking for these microbes must collect them from these extreme environments. Next, they bring them back to the lab and perform tests on the microbes. Studying these samples teaches microbiologists how microbes adapt and survive in extreme conditions.

This microbiologist is collecting soil samples from an active volcano in Antarctica.

Volcanic Microbes

Microorganisms found near volcanoes may help in the fight against global warming. Microbiologists discovered brand-new types of bacteria near a volcano in Italy. They found that the bacteria feed on methane, a main greenhouse gas. Scientists hope to use these bacteria to reduce the amount of methane that's released into the atmosphere.

MARINE MICROBIOLOGISTS

About two-thirds of the planet is covered by water, which is full of microbes. Microbiologists collect microbes from some of the deepest and coldest places in the ocean. These microbes are called marine microbes, and they include bacteria and microalgae, which are one-celled plants that live in water. Marine microbes are so tiny that up to one million microbes can live in just one **milliliter** of seawater!

Marine microbes cannot be raised in a lab, which means microbiologists often head out to sea to complete their studies. Microbiologists are always developing technology to study marine microbes in the deep ocean, because they are very hard to reach.

FUN FACT

MICROBIOLOGISTS HAVE DISCOVERED THAT SOME ZOOPLANKTON, A TYPE OF MICROORGANISM, RELEASE CHEMICALS THAT LIGHT UP IN THE WATER. THIS CAUSES THE WATER AT SOME BEACHES TO GLOW IN THE DARK AT NIGHT.

Marine microbiologists rely on technology like this underwater robot. It is being lifted from the water after taking samples from the ocean floor to test for microbes.

SPACE MICROBES

Could there be life on another planet? Scientists are trying to find out, and microorganisms could hold the answer. Microbiologists study extremophiles to find clues about where to look for life elsewhere. For example, microbiologists discovered a microbe in Antarctica that survives by "eating" air. This suggests that it would be possible for microbes to live on planets where there isn't water, sunlight, or soil.

Microbiologists also study microorganisms found in space. NASA microbiologists collect microorganisms found inside the International Space Station. By studying how they react to conditions in the space station, scientists learn more about how microbes adapt and, in some cases, become harmful.

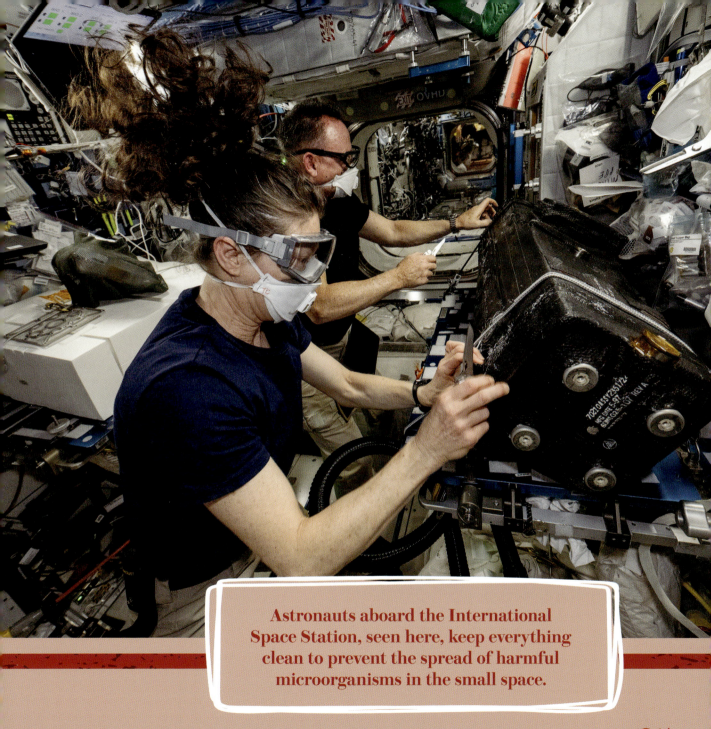

Astronauts aboard the International Space Station, seen here, keep everything clean to prevent the spread of harmful microorganisms in the small space.

SCHOOL DAYS

If microbiology sounds interesting to you, get ready to do a lot of studying! Start by taking science classes, such as physics, biology, and chemistry. In college, future microbiologists will usually choose a science major. After attending a four-year college, they stay in school to get a master's degree. The field's leading scientists often have PhDs as well, which means even more studying. But it's not necessary to have a PhD to get a job as a microbiologist.

During college, you might work as an intern. While interns usually aren't paid, they gain valuable job experience. Universities or research centers often employ interns in their science labs.

Interns are students who work to gain job experience. They can learn a great deal by working in labs with actual microbiologists.

27

A BIG JOB

Once you're ready for a career in microbiology, you can consider working in a variety of places. Hospitals, clinics, and research labs hire microbiologists to learn more about disease-causing bacteria. You might also work with a government organization like the Food and Drug Administration or the Department of Agriculture, ensuring food or drug safety.

The field of microbiology is growing quickly. As it grows, scientists are making exciting new discoveries and advances. If you choose to become a microbiologist, you'll have the opportunity to explore the world of these tiny organisms that have a huge impact on all life on Earth.

FUN FACT

YOU NEED MICROBES IN ORDER TO BREATHE. HALF OF THE OXYGEN ON EARTH COMES FROM MICROBES CALLED PHYTOPLANKTON. THEY TAKE IN CARBON DIOXIDE FROM THE AIR AND GIVE OFF OXYGEN.

Microbiologists play an important role in preventing and treating disease as well as protecting the environment.

GLOSSARY

climate change: Long-term change in Earth's climate, caused mainly by human activities such as burning oil and natural gas.

diagnose: To identify an illness by considering someone's health history and symptoms.

environment: The conditions that surround a living thing and affect the way it lives.

extreme: Great or severe.

identify: To find out the name or features of something.

fermentation: A process by which an organism changes a sugar or starch into an alcohol or acid in the absence of oxygen.

germ: A tiny organism that can cause disease.

microscope: A tool used to view very small objects so they can be seen much larger and more clearly.

milliliter: A unit of measurement equal to about one-fifth of a teaspoon.

mold: A fungus that produces an often fuzzy surface growth especially on damp or decaying matter.

organism: A living thing.

technology: Using science, engineering, and other industries to invent useful tools or to solve problems. Also a machine, piece of equipment, or method created by technology.

volcano: An opening in a planet's surface through which hot, liquid rock sometimes flows.

FOR MORE INFORMATION

Books

Gravel, Elise. *Club Microbe*. Montreal, Quebec, Canada: Drawn & Quarterly, 2024.

Millar, Lindsay. *Wonderful World of the Small: A First Book of Microbiology*. Scotland: Secret Door Press, 2022.

Mould, Steve. *The Bacteria Book: Gross Germs, Vile Viruses, and Funky Fungi*. New York, NY: DK Publishing, 2024.

Websites

American Museum of Natural History: Microbiology
www.amnh.org/explore/ology/microbiology
Learn more about microbiology through games, activities, and videos.

Ducksters: Bacteria
www.ducksters.com/science/bacteria.php
Explore the world of bacteria and then take a quiz to test your knowledge.

Wonderopolis: Can Germs Be Good for You?
wonderopolis.org/wonder/can-germs-be-good-for-you?replytocom=31480
Find out why not all germs are bad and how good bacteria can help your body.

Publisher's note to educators and parents: Our editors have carefully reviewed these websites to ensure that they are suitable for students. Many websites change frequently, however, and we cannot guarantee that a site's future contents will continue to meet our high standards of quality and educational value. Be advised that students should be closely supervised whenever they access the internet.

INDEX

antibiotics, 7

bacteria, 6, 7, 8, 10, 11, 12, 13, 18, 21, 22, 28

cheese, 19

climate change, 4, 16

college, 26

diseases, 4, 6, 11, 12, 13, 14, 15, 19, 28, 29

environmental microbiologist, 16

Fleming, Alexander, 7

food microbiologists, 18, 19

fungi, 6, 8, 12

greenhouse gases, 16, 17

International Space Station, 24, 25

lab, 10, 12, 13, 14, 20, 22, 26, 27, 28

marine microbiologists, 22, 23

master's degree, 26

medical microbiologists, 12

microscope, 5, 10, 11, 12

mold, 7, 8, 9

penicillin, 7

PhD, 26

vaccines, 13, 14, 15

veterinary microbiologist, 14, 15

viruses, 6, 8, 12, 13

volcano, 20, 21

yeast, 8, 18